POOPER
Snooper

by Jennifer Keats Curtis and Julianne Ubigau

illustrated by Phyllis Saroff

"Find it!" shouts Julie.

Sampson is ready. The big black lab mix prances through dust, sand, scrubby brush, and cactus.

With his tail wagging madly and leash
trailing to one side, Sampson sniffs the air.

He darts right

and then dashes left.

He busts through a patch of low shrubs and over straggly vines before slowing. He woofs once, then plops down and stays still.

Julie rushes over and stabs a tiny (practically microscopic) half grain of black rice with a toothpick before putting it into a plastic bag.

"Good boy!" Julie praises, and rewards her mutt by tossing him his most favorite thing in the world—a red ball.

Of course, that speck of rice isn't actually rice. It's poop—Pacific pocket mouse poop.

It's a really big deal that Sampson has discovered it. Not long ago, Pacific pocket mice were believed extinct. Rediscovered in 1993, they were placed on the endangered animal list a year later. The only place in the world these mini mice can be found is in California, and scientists want to learn more about them.

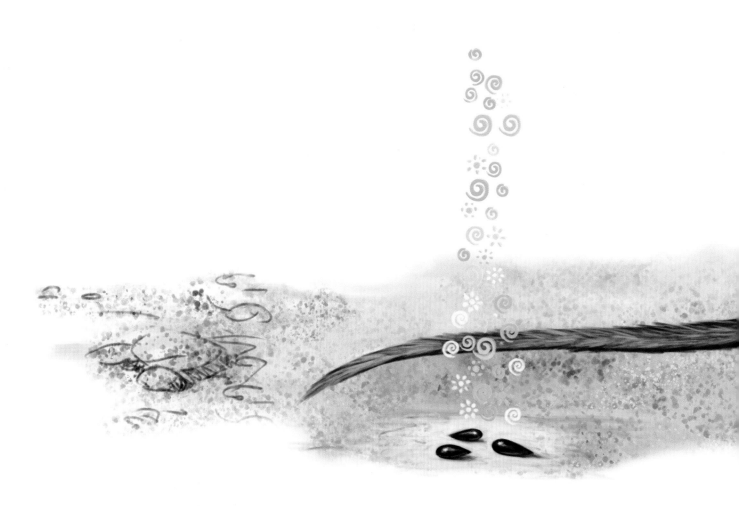

But first, they have to find them.

Sampson is part of a wildlife detective team. He and a few other dogs have been trained as super pooper snoopers. These poop-sniffing pups help scientists track endangered animals.

If the dogs locate the poop, (called scat), scientists don't need to lure and trap these animals. They can learn much of what they need to know by investigating the scat. It's a great way to learn about wildlife with much less stress and bother to the animals.

It's not easy to be a pooper snooper. These are not tracking dogs, nose to the ground, following the scent. Pooper snoopers sniff the air to locate one scent in one place. It takes the right kind of dog with the right personality. One of Sampson's puppy pals flunked out of school. He couldn't ignore the quails and bunnies long enough to complete training.

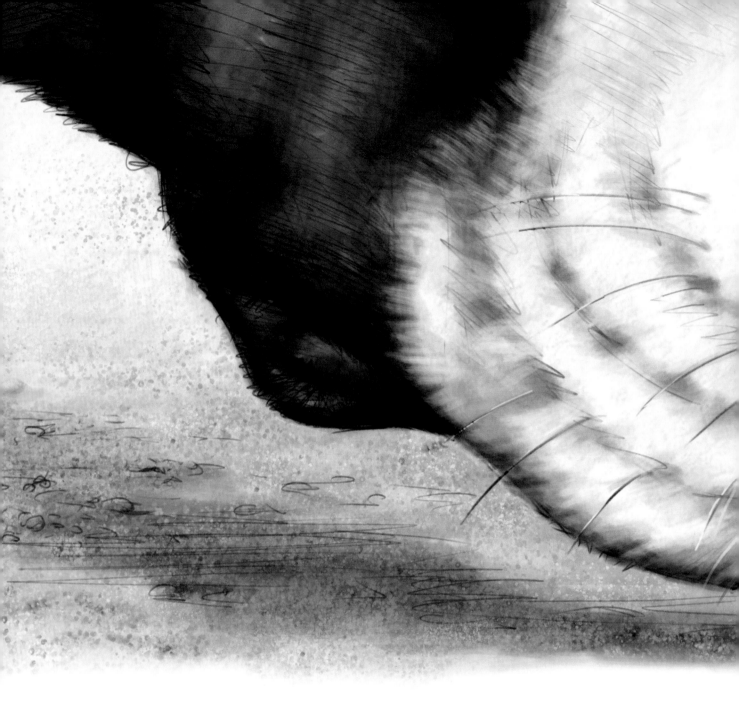

These dog detectives also work long hours, sometimes in difficult conditions. In the case of the pocket mice, not only are their scat super small (about one-third the size of an eyelash); their habitat is sandy.

Sand easily blows through the air—and over the scat—when disturbed. Sampson must be extra cautious not to step in the poop, blow it away with his breath, or get it stuck on the end of his wet nose.

Like most pooper snoopers, Sampson was once a shelter dog, too hyper and ball crazy for families. Yet that energy and ball drive is exactly what makes him such a good dog detective.

He is trained on many species, from salamanders to bears, but his goal is always the same.

Find the scat
and get the
ball.

Before scientists figured out how to use poop-finding pups to find pocket mouse scat, teams of experts shifted sand with tweezers looking for nearly microscopic scat without much luck. Then along came Sampson.

Julie trained him to find Pacific pocket mice poop among the poop of six other kinds of similar mice. His findings have helped scientists discover that these mice have not disappeared. They are just very good at hiding.

Pacific pocket mice are one of 18 kinds of the petite pocket mouse. It's one of the smallest—and most endangered—species in the U.S. The mouse, which would easily fit into your hand, only weighs as much as a coin. Their "pockets" are cheek pouches that the mice fill with seeds while hunting for food. Despite their wee size, pocket mice are important to the environment.

They are considered a keystone species because they can change the ecosystem where they live by breaking up the earth and scattering seeds as they burrow. If there were no more pocket mice, the coastal California landscape might look much different than it does today.

Sampson's training to find pocket mouse scat began with Julie hiding sample scat in small jars. With lots of praise and red-ball rewards, Sampson quickly learned to locate the jars of poop under wood lattice and screens.

After a few days, Sampson sniffed and alerted by sitting at the exact location of a single itty bitty poop under the screen without disturbing it. His reward is always the same. He can hardly wait for Julie to pull the red ball from under her arm and throw it for him.

To teach Sampson
how to find pocket
mice poop in the
field, she buried baby food
jars containing scat in a small area and
asked Sampson to find them.

Over a few days, the search area became broader
until Sampson was searching for scat where
scientists knew the pocket mice lived.

He found pocket mouse poop on his first day!

Sampson might be quite the scientific success, but he's also a sweet pup. At the end of a long scat-sniffing day, Julie pets and brushes him, checking for ticks and cactus spines he picked up in the field.

She lovingly feeds Sampson and then rewards him with, what else?

His red ball!

For Creative Minds

Critically Endangered Pacific Pocket Mouse

The Pacific pocket mouse lives in sandy scrub areas along the coast in California. They used to be found from Tijuana, Mexico to Los Angeles. It was believed that these mice were extinct for over 20 years before a few were found in isolated locations along the coast. Development along the coast and resulting habitat loss is considered the major contributor to these animals being so endangered.

Using information about the Pacific pocket mouse that you have learned, see if you can determine whether the statements below are true or false.

1 Pacific pocket mice are extinct.

2 Pacific pocket mice are the smallest mouse species in the United States.

3 A Pacific pocket mouse would make a great pet.

4 The pockets of these mice are located on their bellies, like kangaroo pouches.

5 Pacific pocket mice are a keystone species.

Answers: 1: False (they are endangered), 2: True, 3: False, 4: False (the pockets are in their cheeks), 5: True

The Dog's Nose Knows

A dog's sense of smell is much better than ours. Dogs even know their humans by smell.

Did you know that dogs can "talk" to each other through their pee and smells? Dogs mark their territories with pee, as if saying, I've been here."

Because dogs have such an incredible sense of smell, they are often trained to help us find things—just like the Pacific pocket mouse poop in this story. Some dogs can help police officers find drugs or warn soldiers of bombs. Other dogs might even use their sensitive noses to alert them to a human's health issues.

Not only is Phyllis Saroff the illustrator of **Pooper Snooper**, but she is also a certified dog trainer. Like Julie and the Conservation Canine handlers, Phyllis understands the importance of helping dogs enjoy training as games or puzzles to be solved. And, she says, even old dogs can learn new tricks! Try playing a nose game with your dog, like Phyllis does with her pup, Spud:

First, make sure your dog knows he needs to pay attention to you by rewarding him for looking up at you. Drop a treat on the ground in front of him. Your dog will eat it and look up at you. When your dog looks up at you, throw the treat off to the side. He will run to find it and come back so you can throw another one in the opposite direction. Make sure you always have a treat ready to reward him.

Let your dog use his wonderful, powerful sense of smell by tossing kibble (dog food) into

the yard like she does for Spud. A dog uses a lot of energy when he searches with his nose. Spud searches in the grass for each tiny piece. He finds each one using only his nose. It takes him about 20 minutes to eat breakfast. He comes inside and flops into his bed to relax until it is time for their morning walk. Some people tell me their dog doesn't have a good sense of smell because they can't find the kibble in the grass. This is not true. All dogs are born with the ability to search with their noses. Given a chance to practice, they can learn nose games very quickly.

Q&A with Scientist Julianne Ubigau

Julianne (Julie) Ubigau is a Research Scientist & Outreach Coordinator at the Conservation Canines Center for Conservation Biology, University of Washington.

How did you become a canine handler?

Rather awkwardly! I interviewed for a job that involved training detection dogs to track moose and wolf scat in Northern Alberta. I was young and had no experience, but I knew I could do it. As part of the interview, I was introduced to a dog named Orion. He was a maniacal lab who lunged at me and quickly robbed a ball from my hand. I was supposed to play fetch. Instead, the interviewers watched Orion run giddy circles around me. I wrestled that dog in the mud for what felt like hours. I never won the ball back. It felt like the worst interview ever. Surprisingly, I got the job. I was hired because I handled the difficult situation with a positive attitude. I didn't get mad, cry, or lose my temper. These dogs are high-energy rescues. If you think you can do something perfectly the first time, this isn't the job for you.

What was your first experience in the field like?

Challenging! There was a lot of snow. I was partnered with Tucker, a black lab mix who didn't like getting his feet wet. I had to teach him to jump off the icy road into deep powder. We would take turns tunneling a path through the snow. We made a good team because we were patient with each other.

How do you describe your work with the dogs?

I think of myself as an interpreter rather than a trainer. This job is all about communication. I'm using my knowledge to help guide them, but my main job is to watch the dog closely, so I know when they have sniffed out a target. It's important to understand your dog's unique personality. For example, Tucker was quiet and needed a cheerleader. I'd dance and sing when he found the target scent. It was exaggerated, but he was motivated by my enthusiasm. With Sampson, I changed the way I worked. He was excitable, so I had to keep him calm enough to concentrate. I muted my enthusiasm and taught him to rest. He was surprisingly sensitive, too. If I appeared frustrated, he'd crawl behind me. When he shut down, I knew I wasn't being a positive co-worker. We'd take a break, play ball, and reset. It was a good reminder for both of us.

What is the most difficult aspect of training?

Our inability to understand the dog's incredible sense of smell. It's a superpower. They're capable of detecting things we don't even know are there so it's difficult to confirm what they are showing us.

What's your favorite part of working with the dogs?

Borrowing their superpowers! It's exciting to explore the forest with a dog who has been trained to detect different scents. It's like putting on special X-ray glasses! I feel privileged to work with someone who is willing to show me what I am unable to see on my own.

Are you working with a dog now?

Yes! Jasper, a giant black lab mix that I rescued. I chose him because he is jovial, easygoing, and great with kids. He is a bundle of energy. The first time I rewarded him for finding scat, he was so excited that he galloped all around the yard like a small pony! He is going to be great at this job.

Do you have advice for our readers who would love to have a job like yours?

Yes! Read a lot and be open, curious, and interested. I enjoy this job because I'm intensely curious. When I was 12, I would come home from school, go outside with Soo, my grandpa's dog, and explore. I'd climb trees, build forts, and save potato bugs. At 37, I'm doing the exact same thing but with purpose! When I was a girl, I didn't know that my hobbies could lead me to a career that I love.

Library of Congress Cataloging-in-Publication Data

Names: Curtis, Jennifer Keats, author. | Saroff, Phyllis V., illustrator.
Title: Pooper snoopers / by Jennifer Keats Curtis and Julianne Ubigau ;
   illustrated by Phyllis Saroff.
Description: Mt. Pleasant, SC : Arbordale Publishing, LLC, [2021] |
   Includes bibliographical references.
Identifiers: LCCN 2021013709 (print) | LCCN 2021013710 (ebook) | ISBN
   9781643518237 (paperback) | ISBN 9781643518374 (adobe pdf) | ISBN
   9781643518510 (epub) | ISBN 9781643518657 (Interactive, read-aloud
   ebook)
Subjects: LCSH: Detector dogs--Juvenile literature. | Tracking
   dogs--Juvenile literature. | Dogs--Sense organs--Juvenile literature. |
   Endangered species--Feces--Detection--Juvenile literature.
Classification: LCC SF428.73 .C87 2021 (print) | LCC SF428.73 (ebook) |
   DDC 636.7/0886--dc23
LC record available at https://lccn.loc.gov/2021013709
LC ebook record available at https://lccn.loc.gov/2021013710

Bibliography
California: A hot spot for Rare Species. U.S. Fish and Wildlife Service Endangered Species Program. April 2013.

Lexile Level: 960L

Printed in the US
This product conforms to CPSIA 2008
First Printing

Arbordale Publishing
Mt. Pleasant, SC 29464
www.ArbordalePublishing.com